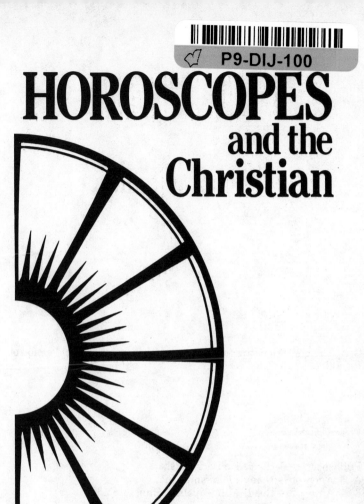

HOROSCOPES
and the
Christian

Robert A.
Morey

BETHANY HOUSE PUBLISHERS
Minneapolis, Minnesota 55438
A Division of Bethany Fellowship, Inc.

P9-DIJ-100

Scripture quotations are taken from the New International Version of
the Bible.

Published by Bethany House Publishers
A Division of Bethany Fellowship, Inc.
6820 Auto Club Road, Minneapolis, Minnesota 55438

Printed in the United States of America

Library of Congress Cataloging in Publication Data

Morey, Robert A., 1946-
  Horoscopes and the Christian.

  Bibliography: p.
  1. Astrology.   I. Title.
BR115.A82M67   261.2'1   81-18092
ISBN 0-87123-202-2 (saddle-bound)   AACR2

Table of Contents

About the Author

Dr. Morey received a B.A. in philosophy from Covenant College, a M.Div. in theology and a D.Min. in cults from Westminster Theological Seminary. He is the East Coast representative of Witness, Inc. He is a frequent contributor to theological journals and has a regular ministry of conference speaking on Christian philosophy, apologetics, the cults and the occult. He is presently pastor of New Life Bible Church in Duncannon, Pennsylvania, and Professor of Apologetics at Perry Bible Institute.

Dr. Morey has also written:

> *How to Answer a Jehovah's Witness*
> *Reincarnation and Christianity*
> *The Bible and Drug Abuse*
> *The Dooyeweerdian Concept of the Word of God*
> *A Christian's Handbook for Defending the Faith*
> *Is Sunday the Christian Sabbath?*
> *An Examination of Exclusive Psalmody*
> *The Saving Work of Christ*
> *The New Life Notebook*
> *The Worship of God*

Introduction

Astrology is big business. There are over 175,000 part-time astrologers and 10,000 full-time astrologers in the U.S. Over 2,000 newspapers carry daily horoscopes! Estimates of American believers in astrology run from 32 million up to one half of the population.

The popularity of astrology can be seen everywhere; and includes astrological T-shirts, jewelry, restaurant place mats, and horoscope vending machines!

The astrology business grosses several hundred million dollars a year. Its future prospects are bright because the products (horoscopes) are meant to be read once and then discarded. New horoscopes must be purchased every day. This complete turnover of merchandise explains why astute financiers are attempting to cash in on the present fad.

What should our attitude be toward astrology? What should we say when someone asks for our astrological sign? Should we read the newspaper horoscopes in the assumption that it is simply innocent fun? Should we wear astrological jewelry? What is astrology all about? Is astrology true?

This book will answer the above questions in order that we can intelligently respond to the astrologers of the twentieth century.

Chapter 1

It Came from Babel, Not the Bible

Astrology is the belief that the destinies of nations and individuals are determined by the relative positions of the stars. These destinies can be discovered by a detailed examination of horoscopes which have been drawn by professional astrologers.

By "astrology" we mean *Western* astrology. Oriental or Chinese astrology has twelve "signs" or animals (i.e., rat, ox, tiger, rabbit, dragon, snake, horse, sheep, monkey, rooster, dog, and pig). Oriental astrology's twelve signs correspond to twelve different *years*, while Western astrology has twelve signs for twelve houses in one year. Since Oriental astrology is not prevalent in the West, and did not adopt Ptolemy's zodiac or calculations, we will not refer to it any further.

Mundane Astrology

Mundane astrology is the practice of predicting the future of a nation. This is the most ancient form of astrology. Many astrologers practiced mundane astrology in ancient Babylon and Egypt.[1]

This earliest form of astrology was connected with the worship of the stars, or *Tsabaistism*.[2] The "stars" were "consulted" and viewed as having power over man because they were assumed to be gods.

This ancient form of planetary worship is the reason God destroyed the Tower of Babel (Gen.11:1-9). The infamous tower was not constructed to reach "unto heaven" as mistakenly translated in the KJV. Rather, archaeologists identify the Tower of Babel as a *ziggurat* or astrological tower on top of which priests could conduct the viewing and worship of the sun, moon, and planets.

The Old Testament and Astrology

The Old Testament Scriptures contain many references to astrological planet worship. The golden calf which Aaron fashioned was the Egyptian astrological god Taurus, the bull (Ex. 32:1-35; Deut. 9:16-21; Neh. 9:18; Ps. 105:19-21; Acts 7:39-43).

During the time of the Kings, the practice of mundane astrology and planetary worship was reestablished in Israel. King Jeroboam made two golden bulls and placed them at Bethel and Dan, saying, " 'Here are your gods, O Israel. . .' " (1 Kings 12:26-29). The prophet of God lamented, "And this thing became a sin; the people went even as far as Dan to worship the one there" (1 Kings 12:30). Astrological worship competed with the worship of YHWH for the hearts of the people.

"The sins of Jeroboam" became a byword. The record of the rise and fall of Israel's and Judah's kings includes whether they allowed the practice of astrology or stopped it (2 Kings 10:28-31).

Israel's final doom was linked directly to its people's involvement with astrological planet worship.

> They forsook all the commands of the Lord their God and made for themselves two idols cast in the shape of calves, and an Asherah pole. They bowed down to all the starry hosts, and they worshiped Baal. They sacrificed their sons and daughters in the fire. They practiced divination and sorcery and sold themselves to do evil in the eyes of the Lord, provoking him to anger.
>
> Therefore the Lord rejected all the people of Israel; he afflicted them and gave them into the hands of plunderers, until he thrust them from his presence. (2 Kings: 17:16, 17, 20)

King Rehoboam of Judah not only erected images of Taurus but also of Aries the goat (2 Chron. 11:15; Lev.17:7). The god Molech (Milchom, Moloch, Malcham) to whom human sacrifices were made was another astrological god who was worshipped (Lev. 18:21; 20:1-6). It represented the sun and was worshipped by casting live children into the fire in its belly.[3]

The worship of Moloch and "Rephan" or Saturn is condemned in Acts 7:43: "You have lifted up *the shrine of Moloch* and *the star of your god Rephan*, the idols you made to worship. Therefore, I will send you into exile beyond Babylon."

When godly kings such as Josiah arose in Israel, they cleansed the nation of the elements of astrology. Several astrological deities are mentioned in the following account:

> The king [Josiah] ordered Hilkiah the high priest, the priests next in rank and the doorkeepers to remove from the temple of the Lord all the articles made for Baal and Asherah and all the starry hosts. He burned them outside Jerusalem in the fields of the Kidron Valley and took the ashes to Bethel. He did away with the pagan priests appointed by the kings of Judah to burn incense on the high places of the towns of Judah and on those around Jerusalem those who burned incense to Baal, to the sun and moon, to the constellations and to all the starry hosts. He took the Asherah pole from the temple of the Lord to the Kidron Valley outside Jerusalem and burned it there. He ground it to powder and scattered the dust over the graves of the common people. He also tore down the quarters of the male shrine prostitutes, which were in the temple of the Lord and where women did weaving for Asherah. (2 Kings 23:4-7)

The Old Testament refers to Israel's frequent involvement in Baal worship nearly one hundred times. Baal was the Phoenician sun-god. Apostate Israel went so far as to build houses dedicated to the worship of the sun (Baal) and even to install horses and chariots dedicated to sun worship (2 Kings 23:11).[4]

The word "asherah," mistranslated as "groves" in the KJV, referred to the Phoenician worship of Venus or the moon as the goddess of love, fertility and good luck.[5] "Asherah" indicates the worship of *Astarte*. C. F. Keil comments,

> Syrophoenician star-worship, in which sun and moon were worshipped under the names of Baal and Astarte as the bearer of the male and female powers of nature, and was pure star worship. . . . The stars were worshipped . . . as the leaders and regulators of sublunary things.
>
> The burning of incense took place not merely to the sun and moon, but also to the signs of the zodiac and to all the host of heaven, i.e., to all the stars (ch. XXIII. 5); by which we are no doubt to understand that the sun, moon, planets and other stars, were worshipped in conjunction with the zodiac, and with this were connected astrology, augury, and the casting of nativities [horoscopes].[6]

The phrase "to the planets" (KJV) or "to the constellations" (NIV) found in 2 Kings 23:5 actually says "twelve signs [of the zodiac]" in the Hebrew! Lange notes that the phrase in the Hebrew refers to "the twelve divisions of the zodiac marked by the figures and names of animals: the twelve constellations of the zodiac."[7]

The Old Testament prophets unanimously condemned planet worship. Jeremiah rejected the worship of "The Queen of Heaven," i.e., the moon (Jer. 7:18; 44:17-25). He prophesied divine judgment upon Israel because of its involvement in astrological worship (Jer. 19:13).

The prophet Ezekiel condemned the men of Israel for worshipping the sun (8:16) and the women of Israel for "mourning for Tammuz" (8:14). Tammuz, or Adonis, "introduced the worship of the seven planets and twelve signs of the zodiac, and . . . was exalted to a god after his death, and honored with a mourning festival."[8] Paintings of the zodiac creatures were actually placed on the walls of the temple and worshipped (8:10-11)!

The wickedness involved was not simply idolatry but *divination* in order to predict the future. Jeremiah warned:

> At that time, declares the Lord, the bones of the kings and officials of Judah, the bones of the priests and prophets, and

the bones of the people of Jerusalem will be removed from their graves. They will be exposed to the sun and the moon and all the stars of the heavens, which they have loved and served and which they have followed and consulted and worshiped. (Jer. 8:1, 2a)

God condemned Israel's involvement in mundane astrology because it was part of the surrounding occult religious world. Israel was forbidden to participate in any occult art by which the future could be predicted.

When you enter the land the Lord your God is giving you, do not learn to imitate the detestable ways of the nations there. Let no one be found among you who sacrifices his son or daughter in the fire, who practices divination or sorcery, interprets omens, engages in witchcraft, or casts spells, or who is a medium or spiritist or who consults the dead. Anyone who does these things is detestable to the Lord, and because of these detestable practices the Lord your God will drive out those nations before you. (Deut. 18:9-12)

The prophet Isaiah singled out the astrologers for special ridicule. They were predicting to the King that Israel would *not* fall, but Isaiah was predicting that it *would*. In this classic confrontation between horoscope and divine revelation, Isaiah declared:

Disaster will come upon you, and you will not know how to conjure it away. A calamity will fall upon you that you cannot ward off with a ransom; a catastrophe you cannot foresee will suddenly come upon you. Keep on, then, with your magic spells and with your many sorceries, which you have labored at since childhood. Perhaps you will succeed, perhaps you will cause terror. All the counsel you have received has only worn you out! Let your astrologers come forward, those stargazers who make predictions month by month, let them save you from what is coming upon you. Surely they are like stubble; the fire will burn them up. They cannot even save themselves from the power of the flame. Here are no coals to warm anyone; here is no fire to sit by. (Isa. 47:11-14)

The Old Testament prophets based their hostility toward astrology on two things: (1) Astrology was a form of polytheism and led to planetary worship. (2) It was an occult art forbidden by Moses on the grounds that they should consult the God of Israel and not the stars if they needed information.

Natal Astrology

Astrology was practiced only for kings and nations until Alexander the Great brought it back to Greece after his conquests. The scientific mind of the Greeks soon redesigned the art into a science that applied to everyone.[9] The chief architect was Ptolemy (A.D. 130).

Ptolemy, in the *Tetrabiblos*, finalized the zodiac and the method of casting horoscopes by the positions of the sun, moon, Mercury, Venus, Mars, Jupiter and Saturn at the time of a person's birth.[10] Once the exact time of a person's birth was known, their future could be predicted. Astrology was no longer only for kings but would now be for the masses as well.

The zodiac is the imaginary belt in the sky across which the planets move in their respected orbits. It is based on observable constellations. The zodiac is divided into twelve houses with 30 degrees in each house. By using the zodiac, the exact position of the seven stars can be calculated at any time. A calendar year is broken down into twelve sections, with dates for each house. For example, if one is born between Oct. 23-Nov. 22, his sign is Scorpio.

Ptolemy's zodiac of seven stars and twelve houses is still used today by the vast majority of astrologers.[11]

The Christian Era

The early church was as hostile to natal astrology as the Old Testament was hostile to mundane astrology. The early converts were encouraged to burn their astrological paraphernalia (Acts 19:18-20).

In the *Didache*, a late first-century or early second-century church manual, we find this warning: "My child, be no dealer in omens, since it leads to idolatry, nor an enchanter, nor an astrologer, nor a magician, neither be willing to look at them; for from all these things idolatry is engendered."[12]

At the Council of Laodicea in A.D. 345 (Canon 36), astrology was forbidden and astrologers were barred from the clergy.

St. Augustine's attack on astrology is well known. He had been a believer in astrology in his non-Christian days. Upon being converted to Christianity he adopted the Bible's hostility to it.[13]

The reintroduction of Greek philosophy (Aristotle) through Thomas Aquinas brought astrology back into favor. As the church grew more corrupt, it turned to the old pagan foundations of Western culture. By the time of the Renaissance, astrology was once again practiced by the royal class and the masses. Astronomy and astrology were viewed as one and the same "science."

The Protestant Reformers followed Augustine's example and viewed astrology as satanic fortune-telling. In Protestant countries, astrology was forbidden by law and condemned by the Church.[14] Even so, astrology continued to flourish. Dr. Dee's relationship to Queen Elizabeth I is still a prime example of the influence of astrologers upon the royal class.[15]

The Scientific Revolution

Although the Protestant churches had failed to break astrology's hold on society, the findings of Copernicus dealt it a tremendous blow.

Ptolemy had developed his zodiac and all his calculations on the assumption that the earth was the center of the universe. He said that the sun, moon, and five planets all circled the earth and focused their "powers" on earth to determine the destiny of every human being.[16]

With the knowledge that the earth was only one of several planets revolving around the sun instead of Ptolemy's earth-centered universe, people began to abandon astrology as an old wives' tale.[17]

The beginning of scientific *astronomy* spelled destruction for *astrology*.

The Occult Revolution

The late nineteenth century witnessed the decline of formal religion due to the secularization of Christianity, and the revival of occult religions such as Theosophy, occult theories such as reincarnation, and occult practices such as astrology.[18]

The *Seattle Daily Times* on Sept. 8, 1975, observed, "History has shown that astrology thrives best in times of religious decline and of social unrest."

Conclusion

Present-day astrology has its roots in the planetary worship of the ancient civilizations of the Fertile Crescent. Its popularity has waxed and waned throughout the centuries. While it suffered serious decline under early Christianity and the rise of modern science, it has returned in strength in the twentieth century.

Chapter 2

The Astrologers Plead Their Case

ARGUMENT NUMBER ONE

"Astrology is true because it is verified by common experience. Those born under the same sign will manifest the same personality traits and probably end up in the same occupations. If a person will only faithfully read his daily horoscope, his day-to-day experience will conform to astrology. Astrologers are able to pick out a person's sign by merely looking at his or her personality."[1]

Examination of Argument

"Common experience" or "personal experience" is a very unreliable standard of proof. Personal or subjective experiences often contradict and therefore refute each other. Nothing can be proven from arguments drawn from subjective personal experience.

According to astrologer Van Deusen, my occupation could not be that of a clergyman, philosopher, college professor, theologian, etc., because I was born under the wrong sign.[2] Thus *my* "personal experience" effectively nullifies the "personal experience" of the astrologers, since my occupation includes all of the above.

If we use an objective scientific test to check the reliability of the astrological personality traits, we find that the empirical evidence is against astrology.

Two pyschologists, Dr. Silverman of Roosevelt University

and Dr. Whitner of Stockton State College, designed a test for the astrological personality traits.

> Silverman and Whitner asked 130 students and faculty to rate themselves on a list of personality traits such as aggressiveness, creativity, ambition and adaptability. Each was asked to name a close friend who was called upon to make similar ratings of the subjects' nature. In addition, each student and faculty member filled out the Eysenck Personality Inventory and provided his exact time and place of birth so that his sun sign, moon sign and ascending sign could be determined. Astrologers consider these the most important influencers of personality. Analyses of the results found no tie between the subjects' self-description, their friends' description or their ratings on the psychological test and characteristics ascribed to them by the horoscopes.[3]

In terms of "common experience" there is also the acid test of *money*. Since the astrologers of the Western world have been practicing their "science" for millenniums, it only stands to reason that they should have gathered all the wealth of the world into their possession. By using astrology, they should have "cleaned up" on the stock and the commodities markets. They should have won every horse race bet. Since they claim that astrology is "true" because it "works," let the financial records of the astrologers be audited.

It is obvious that if astrology *really* worked, the shrewd businessmen of Wall Street would have beaten paths to the astrologers' doors long ago. But, as one Wall Street broker told us, "If you want to lose your money, use astrology to pick stocks."

If astrology is confirmed by experience, what happened to Hitler? Hitler was a devout believer in astrology.[4]

When he addressed the International Congress on Astrology in 1936, he expressed his enthusiasm for astrology and encouraged the astrologers to continue their work.[5]

Historical evidence indicates that the Nazi leaders consulted astrologers for military movements. Eventually their defeats were so terrible that Hitler turned on the astrologers with vengeance. In the April before his death, the astrologers still predicted a good future for Germany and for Hitler!

When viewed objectively, astrology does not verify its claims in common experience. The astrological personality traits are either put forth in synonyms so that all the traits under all the signs are guaranteed to fit everyone or they are inaccurate. There are not twelve basic personalities corresponding to the zodiac.

ARGUMENT NUMBER TWO

"Astrology is true because by it we can predict the future. The great astrologer Nostradamus predicted who would be the new pope. Dr. Dee predicted Queen Elizabeth's accession to the throne. Lily predicted the London fire and the plagues following it. Time after time, the astrologers have been right. Such fulfilled prophecies prove the truthfulness of astrology."[6]

Examination of Argument

The astrologers claim that they have accurately foretold the future in such detail and on so many occasions that their predictions should not be viewed in terms of chance probabilities. This claim must be tested and not simply assumed true. Most books on astrology list only the "success stories" and never admit any failures.

Astrological predictions must not be so vague as to be guaranteed fulfillment somewhere by someone at some time. Such statements as, "There will be many divorces next year," hardly qualify as verifiable predictions. It is an inviolate law that *a prediction which can be fulfilled by anything cannot be validated by anything.*

Cavendish comments:

> The wooliness of astrological language is one of the reasons for the failure of astrologers to agree on the interpretation of a

given set of planetary positions. The fact that many astrological predictions are so all-embracing that they can scarcely fail to come true is also due to the vagueness of the astrologer's language as well as to his natural caution.[7]

The daily horoscope predictions are so vague that any prediction under any sign will "seem" to be fulfilled. One newspaper editor discovered this fact and used it to save money.

> The inanity of horoscopes was demonstrated indirectly by the editor of a large daily newspaper who was forced to publish an outdated version when the new material failed to arrive in time for publication. Not one of the 100,000 readership complained of any irrelevance so the editor concluded he could spare himself the cost of new horoscopes and repeat the old ones.[8]

As an experiment, we cut off the identifying sign for each prediction and had people try to find the prediction which described their day. Once they had their prediction, we identified what prediction went with what sign. Virtually no one had chosen their sign and nearly all felt several predictions described their day.

The argument that a *fulfilled* prediction *proves* astrology logically means that a *failed* prediction *disproves* astrology. Some astrologers try to avoid the above principle by saying, "When the prediction comes true, this proves astrology. If it fails, this is due to the fact that the stars do not compel but only impel. The people did not cooperate with the stars. Thus unfulfilled predictions are irrelevant." In this way they guarantee that they cannot fail!

Actually, since the astrologers have offered the fulfillment of their predictions as the "proof" of their system, unfulfilled predictions are valid arguments against the system.

Unfulfilled Astrological Predictions

Fulfilled predictions are listed in great detail by such astrologers as Russell and Glass. We need to set the record straight by a corresponding list of predictions which have failed. The following examples are some of the astrological predictions which uncontestably failed.

1. In A.D. 1524 an alignment of the planets occurred. This event occurs repeatedly and will occur again in 1982. Astrologers predicted that all sorts of catastrophes would befall the world (floods, earthquakes, fires, etc.). People fled to the mountains as the date approached. Nothing extraordinary happened.[9]

2. Bonatto, a renowned thirteenth-century astrologer, did not accurately predict his own death.[10]

3. The astrologer Galileo in 1609 drew up a horoscope for the Duke of Tuscany which indicated that the Duke would enjoy a long life. The Duke died two weeks later.[11]

4. Astrologers drew a horoscope for the French philosopher Voltaire which placed his death at age 32. When Voltaire was 60 years old, he published a pamphlet "apologizing" that his age disproved astrology.[12]

5. Astrologers were not able to predict the outbreak of World War II. Furthermore, when it started, they said that England would not participate.[13]

6. During World War II various newspapers in England tabulated astrologers' predictions concerning the course of the war and its ultimate outcome. The astrological predictions failed to materialize.[14]

7. Hitler used astrology in his attempt to gain military supremacy. He failed to achieve his goal and suffered a dismal death.[15]

8. A modern astrologer, Manly Palmer Hall, stated that since the U.S. would be in a Sagitarian cycle during 1960-1980, the nation would experience amazing progress and lead in the social and intellectual life of the world. Sad to say, the U.S. declined from 1960-1980.[16]

9. The astrologers failed to predict President Kennedy's assassination, and had predicted his re-election instead.[17]

10. The Communist government in China was to fall from power by 1970.[18]

11. The "Reluctant Prophet," Daniel Logan, predicted that the Viet Nam war would continue from 1965-1985 and that the U.S. and Russia would become allies against China before 1980.[19]

12. Astrologers predicted that California would fall into the sea in 1969. California remains intact.[20]

Many other unfulfilled predictions could be cited,[21] but these twelve examples are enough to challenge sufficiently the reliability of astrology to predict the future.

Nostradamus

Nearly all pro-astrology books refer to Nostradamus as the example *par excellente* of astrologers' ability to predict the future. Since his prophecies have been gathered and translated into one volume,[22] we can easily check the accuracy of his predictions.

The reading of Nostradamus' prophecies substantiates Mackay's comment that Nostradamus' prophecies "take so great a latitude, both as to time and space, that they are almost sure to be fulfilled somewhere or other in the course of a few centuries."[23]

Even Nostradamus admitted that his prophecies were vague. His only defense was to claim that he *could* have given exact dates and details but did not *wish* to do so!

The translator H. Roberts complicates matters by juggling facts and dates in an attempt to save Nostradamus from faulty predictions. But if one examines with care the few predictions where Nostradamus did give specific dates, one will find that Nostradamus failed to predict future events accurately:

1. He predicted that by 1792 Venice, Italy, would become a great power and influence in the world.[24] Venice is still waiting for this to happen.

2. The downfall of the Catholic clergy in A.D. 1609 which he predicted never materialized.[25]

3. Nostradamus predicted that in A.D. 1792, persecution against the Catholic church would rise. It would be more severe than the persecution against the Church in North Africa. Because the Church in North Africa ceased to exist, the continued presence of the Catholic church seems to refute Nostradamus' prediction.[26]

4. Astrologers were to be persecuted in A.D. 1607. This never happened.[27]

5. By A.D. 1700, China "would subdue the whole northern section" of the world.[28]

Since the above predictions as they stand are failures, Mr. Roberts attempts to add years to the dates. For example, the astrologers were to be persecuted in 1607 according to Nostradamus. Roberts says that Nostradamus really meant 1932. But one fails to see any reason for such manipulations. Nostradamus' prediction also failed in 1932.[29]

Predictions Concerning the Weather

Astrologers have for centuries claimed the ability to predict the weather. But do their predictions come true?

Peco della Mirandola in the sixteenth century decided to test the astrological weather forecasts. His conclusion is interesting:

> I have been taking notes of weather conditions for a whole winter and checking them against predictions. On the 130 days or more that I made my observations, there were only six or seven which agreed with the published prediction.[30]

Modern research into the reliability of astrological weather forecasting has validated Mirandola's conclusion.[31] The meterologists' computers have a better average of success than do the astrologers' horoscopes.

ARGUMENT NUMBER THREE

"Astrology was practiced by the authors of the Bible. After

all, how did Noah predict the flood, and how did the prophets prophesy? They used astrology. As a matter of fact, the Hebrews were the astrologers of the ancient world. The "three wise men" were astrologers. Therefore, the Bible supports astrology." [32]

Examination of Argument

The Astrologers' Ignorance of the Bible

Our study in chapter one of the history of astrology reveals clearly that the biblical authors condemned all forms of astrology. The Old Testament prophets attributed the ultimate destruction of Israel as a nation to the national involvement in mundane astrology and planetary worship. With such clear teaching of the Bible in mind, it is astounding that astrologers attempt to place the Bible on their side!

Russell claims that there is nothing about astrology in the Old Testament, but then asserts that the biblical prophets were astrologers![33] He also says that astrology "was never formally proscribed by the church."[34] Evidently, he did not know of Canon 36 of the Council of Laodicea, which forbids such practices (see ch. 1).

Attempting to involve the early church in astrology, Russell points to the astrological practices of a Greek mystery religion called "Gnosticism." However, the authors of the New Testament clearly denounced Gnosticism as a pagan religion.[35] Russell fails to manifest even a minimal knowledge of church history or Scripture.

The same can be said of J. Goodavage who placed in bold print, "How Ancient Biblical Disasters Were Foreseen,"[36] and "The Great Biblical Prophets Were Astrologers."[37]

He even says that "the Bible is full of" astrology.[38]

In the "Your Personal Problem Department," *The Horoscope Guide* (June, 1980, p. 8), Georgina Tyler is asked by L. H., "Does the Bible give references to astrology in many instances? If so, where will I find them?"

Georgina's answer is, "The Bible verifies astrology in many instances."

She said Isa. 47:13-14 "verified" astrology. However, she failed to realize that this reference *condemns* Israel for practicing astrology. Isaiah warns the astrologers that they and their predictions will be destroyed.

We are thus faced with astrologers who claim that the Bible never mentions astrology (Russell) and those who claim that the Bible is full of it (Goodavage). Generally Bible references are quoted out of context and made to say the exact opposite of the intent of the author.

The attempt to justify astrology by calling it "biblical" and by stating it was accepted by the early church is utterly refuted by the biblical and historical evidence. The Bible, the Judaism of the Old Testament and the Christianity of the New Testament are united in their opposition to any form of astrology.

The Wise Men

Many astrologists assume that the Magi of Matthew 2 were astrologers and that they found their way to the infant Christ by means of a horoscope.[39] But the evidence is strongly against this assumption.

First, the "star" was *not* the conjunction of Jupiter and Saturn or Jupiter and Venus or any other planets.[40] The bright light suddenly appeared, moved, disappeared, reappeared and remained stationary according to Matt. 2:2, 7, 9. This is hardly the behavior of a planet or star. It was very likely a supernatural phenomenon.

Secondly, the Magi were probably not pagan astrologers but Gentile converts to Judaism who understood Balaam's statement in Num. 24:17: "A *star* will come out of Jacob and a *sceptre* shall rise out of Israel." This prophecy had been interpreted for centuries as referring to the coming of the Messiah.

This also explains why King Herod turned to the Old Testament rather than call the astrologers to find out where the Messiah was to be born.

> When King Herod heard this he was disturbed, and all Jerusalem with him. When he had called together all the people's chief priests and teachers of the law, he asked them where the Christ was to be born. In Bethlehem in Judea, they replied, for this is what the prophet has written: "But you, Bethlehem, in the land of Judah, are by no means least among the rulers of Judah; for out of you will come a ruler who will be the shepherd of my people Israel." (Matt. 2:3-6)

Lastly, the Magi did not use astrology to discern the evil intent of Herod. An angel warned them to flee (Matt. 2:12). There is no mention of horoscopes in the passage.

ARGUMENT NUMBER FOUR

"Astrology can be demonstrated by studying the case histories of astro-twins, i.e., people born at exactly the same moment. People with identical horoscopes will live parallel lives and experience many things in common. This is proof of the validity of astrology."[41]

Examination of Argument

J. Goodavage has done more to promote this argument for astrology than anyone else. He lists multiple examples of astro-twins whose lives supposedly run parallel to each other.

The evidence presented by Goodavage seems impressive until one tries to research his examples. He does not present any documentation to verify his claims.

Keith Eriksen decided to investigate the case histories of some of Goodavage's astro-twins. His research has placed a question mark over Goodavage's accuracy and methodology. The following is an example of what Eriksen found as he investigated several case histories Goodavage set forth.[42]

CASE NO. 1 (*Horoscope*, May, 1976):

> Donald Chapman and Donald Brazill were born in Cali-

fornia. Each boy came into the world at almost the same moment on September 5, 1933, in neighboring towns about twenty-four miles apart.

Five days after their twenty-third birthday on September 10, 1956, Don Brazill of Ferndale and Don Chapman of Eureka met for the first and last time in this life. They were driving in opposite directions on U.S. Highway 101 south of Eureka early on a Sunday morning after taking their girlfriends (who live in each other's hometown!) home when their cars crashed head-on. Both were killed instantly—decapitated.

FACTS

1. Photocopies of birth certificates reveal that Donald Brazill was born at 12:10 p.m. and Donald Chapman at 8:30 a.m. This is hardly "at almost the same moment."

2. They were not decapitated! Death certificates indicate that Brazill died of a crushed skull, and Chapman of a cerebral hemorrhage.

CASE NO. 2 (*Astrology: The Space Age Science*, p. 32):

In 1939 two unrelated women met for the first time in a hospital room in Hackensack, N.J. Their last names were Hanna and Osborne, but they had the same first name—Edna. Each woman had a baby at the same time; the babies weighed the same and were given the same name—Patricia Edna.

Just another coincidence? Maybe, but here's what their conversation revealed. Both their husbands were named Harold. Each Harold was in the same business and owned the same make, model, and color car. The Hannas and Osbornes had been married exactly three and a half years and had the same anniversary. The babies were their first. Both fathers were born in the same year, month, and day. The mothers too had the same birth date—and the same number of brothers and sisters. Each Edna was a blue-eyed brunette, same height, same weight and wore the same kinds of clothes. Their husbands were of the same religion, a different one than that of the wives, which was also the same. Each family owned a dog named Spot, same mixed breed, same size, and the same age. Both Spots were bought at the same time and were of the same sex.

FACTS (obtained from Mrs. H. B. Hanna)

1. The babies were born over one hour apart.
2. The fathers were not in the same business.
3. The fathers did not own the same make, model, and color of car.
4. Both couples did not have the exact same marriage anniversary.
5. The fathers were not born on the same day, month, and year.
6. The mothers did not share the same birth date.

CASE NO. 3 ("The Strange Mystery of Astro-Twins," *Science and Mechanics*, March 1967):

It seems that every astrologer in New York City was aware of the fact that the city's former two top commissioners—Police: Michael J. Murphy, and Fire: Edward Thompson, were born within an hour of each other on July 19, 1913, in the same neighborhood of Queensborough. . . .

Each man attended many of the same schools at the same times, including Brooklyn Law School. Both graduated in 1936, but from then on . . . a 12-month interval separated major, similar events in their careers.

Thus when Commissioner Thompson resigned to take another post, it seemed . . . by use of astrology, that Police Commissioner Murphy would be out of office within the year. It worked out in the most uncanny way, right on the click of the planetary "dials," you would say.

FACTS (obtained from Edward Thompson)

1. Mr. Thompson says that no one knows the exact time of his birth.
2. Mr. Thompson graduated from Brooklyn Law School in 1936, but Michael Murphy graduated in 1938.

CASE NO. 4 (*Astrology: The Space Age Science*, p. 33):

On March 30, 1964, a doctor and his wife were sentenced to two years in prison in Tucson, Arizona, for extreme cruelty to their five-year-old adopted daughter, Tina. The child was found by the housekeeper, beaten, bloody and half-starved.

Her hands were tightly roped behind her back and she cowered behind the furnace room in the basement. . . .

At almost the same time, but in another state, an identical story unfolded. A dentist and his wife had beaten and brutalized their five-year-old adopted daughter and kept her tied up in the basement of their home. They too were sentenced.

The second child was Tina's twin sister from whom she had been separated since infancy!

FACTS (obtained from *Tucson Star* newspaper reference—librarian)

1. Tina's twin was a brother (fraternal twin).
2. The twin brother died over one and a half years before Tina was found badly beaten.
3. The twin brother had not been separated from the family. (The dentist and wife were fabrications.)

CASE NO. 5 ("The Strange Mystery of Astro-Twins," *Science and Mechanics*, March 1967):

In Philadelphia's Jefferson Medical College, Drs. Thomas D. Duane and Thomas Behrendt performed an exciting experiment with 15 sets of twins. In separate, brilliantly lit rooms, the twins were wired to electro-encephalograph machines which produced a perfectly identifiable brain-wave pattern called the Alpha rhythm. One twin was told to blink his eyes each time he was asked. The other twin of course had no idea what was going on and wasn't told anything about the experiment's purpose. Yet in almost all cases, the twin who did nothing at all registered the identical brain wave "sent" by the twin who was blinking his eyes!

FACTS (obtained from Dr. T. Duane, M.D.)

Results showed only 2 out of 15 sets of twins registered identical brain waves.

In the light of the above investigation, we cannot accept Mr. Goodavage's case histories as scientifically reliable or as "proofs" of astrology.

Gauquelin studied over 50,000 horoscopes, many of them of

"astro-twins," to see if there is any evidence for parallel lives among time twins. He did not find any evidence of parallelism. He did find the following evidence against astrology:

> None of the astrologers we studied passed the classic test known as "the test of opposed destinies." The test consists of forty birth dates, twenty of well-known criminals and twenty of persons who led a long and peaceful life. The astrologer's task is to separate the two groups of people on the basis of their birth horoscope. The result is always great confusion; the astrologers invariably select a mixed bag of criminals and peaceful citizens in about the same proportions that a machine would by picking randomly. We should add that only sincerely believing astrologers agreed to take our test in the first place; the immense majority of charlatans always find a likely excuse to avoid a confrontation that might endanger their credibility in the public eye.[43]

ARGUMENT NUMBER FIVE

"Astro-physics has finally proven the validity of astrology. We can now measure the astrological forces which determine our destinies. Dr. Takata has shown that albumin increases in human blood during sun spots.[44] We can now measure the effect of the sun's radiation.[45] The gravitational and tidal force of the moon on insects, animals, and man is now clear.[46] Dr. Brown demonstrated that oysters open and close according to the tidal force of the moon.[47] Science has at last proven astrology to be true."

Examination of Argument

No one questions the *physical* effect of sunspots on the ionosphere sixty miles above the earth or on the amount of albumin in human blood. The tidal and gravitational force of the moon does effect certain changes in insects, animals, and man. The documentation for these things is increasing as new instruments are invented which can measure the effect of the sun and moon on the earth.

While these things are true, there is no logical connection between astrology and the findings of astro-physics. The argument of the astrologers at this point commits the "Fallacy of Four Terms" (Quaternis Terminorum). They are referring to facts which do not have anything to do with the position they wish to prove.

First, the concept of astrology requires a *special* influence from seven zodiac heavenly bodies. The evidence reveals only *general* influences from the sun and moon.

Second, astrology requires that the "stars" above produce *permanent* and *unchangeable* effects in animals and man. The evidence shows that the effect from the sun and moon are only *temporary* and *changeable*. The amount of albumin returns to normal once the sunspots have disappeared.

Third, astrology requires that the influence from above affect the destiny of *certain individuals* (babies) and at *only one time in the life of that individual* (birth). The evidence demonstrates that the radiation from the sun and the tidal force of the moon are *universal* and *constant*.

Fourth, astrologers teach that while the sun and moon rule over the body and the soul, the positions of *the five planets of the zodiac* are more important in drawing horoscopes. In spite of this, the evidence they point to refers *only* to the sun and moon. Where is the evidence for any *influencial* radiation and tidal affects of Mercury, Mars, Jupiter and Saturn?

When the astrologers appeal to the physical and measurable effects of the sun's radiation and the moon's gravity, this actually means that the measurable radiation and gravity of the five planets should be examined. Since they appeal to such evidence to indicate that the sun and moon do influence us in certain ways, then we can appeal to the same kind of evidence which reveals that the five planets do *not* affect us.

Mars and the M.D.

Which has the greater gravitational force and tidal effect

upon an infant at birth: the five distant zodiac planets or the doctor who delivered the baby? Lee Ratzan has calculated that the doctor has a greater gravitational and tidal effect on the infant than does Mars. At the moment of birth, when the physician hovers over the child, his gravitational and tidal force is greater than any of the five zodiac planets.[48] Dr. Carl Sagan also came up with the same mathematical fact.[49]

Dr. Abell has pointed out:

> The tidal force produced on a man by the planet Mars when it is at its nearest to the earth is about 50 million times less than the tidal force on the same man produced by the typical Sunday copy of the *Los Angeles Times* lying on a table six feet away.[50]

By using the argument of *measurable* physical effects, the astrologers are opening themselves up to scientific refutation. This is why some astrologers are now saying that the influence of the stars is on a spiritual, "astral" level and *not* on a physical level.[51]

ARGUMENT NUMBER SIX

"Various statisical studies clearly show that the horoscope of an individual determines that person's destiny, personality and the kind of occupation he will probably enter. For example, M. Gauquelin has shown that Mars was strong in the horoscope of soldiers and athletes."

Contrary Statistical Studies

Astrology claims that people born under the same sign will manifest certain characteristics of personality and temperament and will gravitate toward certain careers. For example, those born under Libra will be artistic because Venus, the planet of art and beauty, rules Libra. We must check the birth times and astrological signs of people involved in various careers. If astrology is true, then we will find that certain signs predominate in certain careers more than in other careers.

1. Let us begin with painters and musicians. Are their numbers predominately Libras? One scientist, a Mr. Farnsworth, "has had the patience to study the birth dates of more than two thousand famous painters and musicians. . . . The supposed correlation does not exist; in fact, chance made the correlation come out negative; that is, Libra had fewer than its quota of artists."[52]

2. If we take the *American Men of Science*, and examine the birth times of the people listed, are the majority of one sign?

> Astronomer J. Allen Hynek studied the birth dates of scientists included in *American Men of Science*. The distribution of the dates according to zodiacal signs fell into a random pattern. Seasonal variations in the number of births, which as Huntington has discovered occur in every population, were also found by Hynek; but these have nothing to do with astrology.[53]

Dr. Bok did the same research using *"Who's Who in Science"* and came to the same conclusion.[54]

3. According to astrology, Mars is connected with violence and death. It must therefore be present in the majority of horoscopes of criminals.

One researcher examined the horoscopes of 623 murderers to see if Mars was predominant in their horoscopes.

> Therefore we obtained the vital statistics of all French criminals on record at the Paris Courthouse. We selected the files of 623 murderers who, according to the judgment of experts, were the most notorious in the annals of justice for the horror of their crimes. Most of them died under the guillotine. When their horoscopes were cast, it was shown that Mars was not particularly strong among these arch-criminals.
>
> The positions of Mars are evenly distributed among the twelve astrological houses, following the random pattern very closely; none of the figures differs significantly from the theoretical numbers expected by chance. It is rather disappointing for astrological theory. . . .[55]

4. Barth and Bennett checked for the predominance of

Mars among military men and found no evidence of the "Mars effect."[56]

Favorable Statistical Studies

The astrologers, prone to dismiss the kinds of statistical studies which we have just reviewed, present statistical studies which *they* have done. What can we say of these favorable studies?

First of all, the vast majority of the statistical studies done by astrologers lack any scientific merit or credence.

The American Association of Scientific Societies investigated the studies put forth by astrologers. Their conclusion was that "none of the influences alleged by the astrologers was verified."[57]

Even M. Gauquelin had to admit:

> Our first task was to evaluate the statistical methods employed by the astrologers themselves. Their techniques were found to be severely limited: the laws of chance are ignored and conclusions are reached without support.[58]

Robur, a Swiss astrologist, claimed that his survey of 2,817 musicians revealed that the sun's position at their birth indicated that they would have musical ability. Paul Conderc, an astronomer at the Paris Observatory, decided to investigate Robur's statistical study. Conderc concludes:

> The position of the sun has absolutely no musical significance. The musicians are born throughout the entire year on a chance basis. NO sign of the zodiac or fraction of a sign favors or does not favor them. We conclude: the assets of scientific astrology are equal to zero, as is the case with commercialized astrology.[59]

The "Mars Effect"

Nearly all of the statistical studies put forth by astrologers are either unscientific or inaccurate. However, the work of M. Gauquelin concerning the "Mars Effect" on soldiers and athletes deserves special attention. Astrologers rely strongly on his research into the "Mars Effect." He claimed that Mars predominated in the horoscopes of the soldiers and athletes he selected for research.

Gauquelin has repeatedly stated that his research does *not* prove astrology.[60] Despite this, astrologers quote Gauquelin's work as if it does prove astrology. Gauquelin and others feel that his research does *not* prove astrology because classical astrology is based on Ptolemy's rules and calculations found in the *Tetrabiblos*. Gauquelin's work does not consistently correspond to Ptolemaic rules of prediction. His findings were a surprise to astrologers as well as to astronomers.

Gauquelin's work is increasingly suspect because scientists have raised serious doubts about Gauquelin's basic statistical assumption, his use of binomial probability statistics, his selection of date, lack of outside verification, etc.[61]

Even if his study of the "Mars Effect" on soldiers and athletes is validated at some time in the future, this has nothing to do with astrology and the position of the sun, moon and other planets at the time of the birth of these people. Gauquelin found *no* "Mars Effect" for criminals and *no* "Libra Effect" on musicians.[62] His findings in these areas should cause astrologers to hesitate before claiming that Gauquelin's work proves astrology.

Conclusion

We have examined six popular arguments for astrology and have found them lacking any merit or validity. The burden of proof still rests squarely upon the shoulders of the astrologers. Until they can produce empirical facts and solid reasoning, astrology must be considered a faith devoid of any foundation, whether it be experience, ability to predict the future, the Bible, studies of time twins, astro-physics, or statistical studies. Astrology has been weighed and found wanting.

Chapter 3

Science and Astrology: Horoscope vs. Telescope

Modern astrologers refer to themselves as astro-scientists, astro-biologists, scientific astrologers, etc., and have repeatedly claimed that science has proven the validity of astrology. Therefore, it is only proper to take a scientific look at astrology.

The Problems with Ancient Astrology

An Erroneous Assumption

Ancient astrology *is a system of belief which is based solely on what the unaided human eye can see.* The ancient astrologers assumed that *"appearance" always corresponds to reality.* Therefore its foundational concepts and starting principles were in error.

As Ptolemy looked around, he concluded that the earth was the center of the universe, that the sun, moon, planets and stars all revolved around the earth. According to what he *saw with his eyes*, the sun came up in the east and set in the west.

A Religious Foundation

Ptolemy's geo-centered universe was not just a physical phenomenon. It had its roots in a *mystical* or *religious* world view which saw man as the center of the intelligence, will, and emotion of the universe. The universe existed for man and focused all its cosmic energies on man. The thought that there could be intelligent life somewhere else or that the energy of the universe could be focused someplace else never crossed Ptolemy's mind.

These ideas formed the basis of Ptolemy's astrology. Why else could he talk about the stars as choosing man's destiny, or assume that the stars could choose anything or that man was important enough to be chosen?

We can therefore understand why Copernicus' theory that the sun was the center of this galaxy and that the earth revolved around it, at first shattered people's confidence in astrology. Copernicus had actually attacked the foundational religious concept of astrology that man was the center of the universe. The astrology-riddled medieval church condemned his view as heresy.

Confidence in astrology was also weakened because Copernicus said that appearance may *not* correspond to reality. In other words, just because our eyes *see* the sun move through the sky does *not* mean that the sun is moving at all. In reality, the earth is moving and the sun is standing still.

Copernicus' helio-centered universe overthrew the foundational principle by which horoscopes were drawn.

Copernicus' teaching did not destroy astrology in his own day. Neither are modern astrologers affected by Copernicus' helio-centered universe, because astrology is ultimately based on Ptolemy's religious convictions and not on science or reality. This is why the modern claim that astrology is a *science* is so absurd. Without its religious foundation, astrology cannot exist.

The New Planets

A second problem is created by the assumption that "appearance" always corresponds to reality. Using only the human eye, Ptolemy saw only the sun, moon, Mercury, Venus, Mars, Saturn and Jupiter. He assumed that *there were no other planets in our galaxy.* Using the positions of the seven *visible* stars, he set forth in the *Tetrabiblos* the calculations which are to be used in drawing up a person's horoscope.

Uranus was discovered in 1781, Neptune in 1846, and Pluto in 1930. Since these planets were not included in Ptolemy's horoscope calculations, they threaten to annul *all* of the horoscopes which follow his calculations!

The problem of the discovery of new planets has provoked astrologers into making absurd statements. Goodavage "solves" the problem of Uranus, Neptune, and Pluto by stating that they came into existence just before they were discovered![1]

Other astrologers have proposed that until Uranus, Neptune, and Pluto were discovered, they had no part in determining our destiny or controlling our lives. But *now* these planets are a vital part of astrology![2]

West and Tooner suggest that Uranus, Neptune, and Pluto are not important because they affect only a few outstanding people and have no influence on the masses.[3]

Uranus, Neptune, and Pluto will always prove an embarrassment to the astrologers because their entire system of drawing horoscopes is based on Ptolemy's seven-star zodiac.

The Constellations

Ptolemy's zodiac is actually based on constellations which are only *optical illusions*. One look through a telescope shows that constellations such as Leo or Pisces or Sagittarius do not actually exist. Stars which were unseen by human eyes appear and disrupt the imaginary lines of the animals, men, and objects which supposedly make up the constellations. In no way can Ptolemy's zodiac be considered scientific.

There is another reason why the zodiac is an illusion. The positions of the constellations relative to the earth have changed. Cavendish explains:

> On March 21 each year astrologers say that the sun is in Aries. In reality, the sun is not in the constellation Aries

(though it was 2,000 years ago) but is in the constellation Pisces. When an astrologer today says that the sun is in one sign of the zodiac it is really in the preceding sign.[4]

Astrologers are in a dilemma at this point. Ptolemy's zodiac is based on the assumption that the constellations are *real* and *fixed* while they are actually *imaginary* and *moving.*

Because of these facts, modern astrologers state that their zodiac is *not* based on the constellations. But when they do this they unwittingly cut the zodiac from any correspondence to reality. Either way they lose.

A Tropical Zodiac

Ptolemy assumed that the earth was flat and that everyone on it saw the same stars he did. Thus he developed a "tropical" zodiac which works only if one can see what point of the zodiac is ascending on the horizon. But above 60 degrees latitude, one cannot see what point of the zodiac is ascending and thus no horoscope can be drawn.[5]

This means that while horoscopes can be drawn for people living in Greece where Ptolemy lived, no horoscopes can be drawn for people living in Alaska, Northern Canada, Finland, Siberia, etc.!

Ptolemy's astrology is therefore geographically limited and thus invalid because it does not take into account the people living above 60 degrees latitude. Are we to believe that these people escape the influence of the zodiac and are free from the horoscope?

Anthropomorphic Polytheism

Ptolemy's astrology was directly based upon the religious presupposition of planetary worship. The stars were viewed as gods who manifest intelligence, emotions, and will. The stars knew what was best and wisely chose each person's destiny. They were capable of anger (Mars) or love (Venus). They looked down upon man, favoring one man and disfavoring another. Ever since Ptolemy, the astrologers have consistently attributed human characteristics to the stars (e.g., Saturn is viewed as evil).

While some astrologers have ignored or denied the obvious polytheistic structure, language, and rationale of astrology, some, like best-selling author Linda Goodman, have actually suggested a return to polytheistic planet worship.[6] In this light, how can astrology claim to be scientific?

The Precession of the Equinoxes

Ancient astrology assumed that the earth's axis of rotation *always* pointed directly toward the star Polaris and *never* moved. This star marks the North Celestial Pole. In order to begin the calculations for drawing horoscopes, astrologers must obtain a fix from the day of the vernal equinox or the day spring begins. Without this fix, no horoscope can be drawn. But now the truth can be told:

> The earth moves in a *counterclockwise* direction, making a complete circle once a year . . . the North Pole describes its own *clockwise* circle, the equinoctical point also advances in a clockwise direction. This means that it moves backwards at a rate of one degree for every 72 years. . . . Therefore with the equinoctical point progressing 1/72 of a degree, Spring arrives 1/72 of a day or 20 minutes earlier each year. . . . This is why the phenomenon is called the Precession of the Equinoxes.[7]

Ptolemy assumed that the equinox was *fixed* and *never varied*. In reality it *moves* and *varies*! No wonder Gauquelin stated: "It is the discovery of the precession of the equinoxes that threatens astrology at its very foundation, namely the signs of the zodiac."[8]

Since the signs of the zodiac are determined by the equinoxes, the backward march of the equinoxes means that we all must move one sign backward in the zodiac. Those who *thought* they were born under Cancer were really born under

Leo! We have all been reading the wrong horoscope columns because we all have been told the wrong signs!

Cavendish says: "When an astrologer today says that the sun is in one sign of the zodiac it is really in the preceding sign, which seems to cast some doubt on all astrological findings for several hundred years past."[9]

The vast majority of astrologers today refuse to recognize the precession of the equinoxes. But a small group of astrologers has developed a moving zodiac which identifies an "Aries" as really being a "Pisces." They have developed a sidereal zodiac in opposition to Ptolemy's fixed tropical zodiac.

These two warring camps of astrologers go to great lengths to refute each other's horoscopes! The sidereal astrologers prove that the Aries person actually manifested Piscean traits. The tropical astrologers prove that the Arian person manifested Arian traits! Who is right? We would suggest, *neither.*

We should notice one other thing about the attitude of the astrologers toward the precession of the equinoxes. They usually appeal to it when they want to prove that we are now in the Aquarian age. However, they repudiate it when antagonists bring it up.[10]

We fail to see how it is valid to use the precession of the equinoxes whenever it suits one but to reject it when it is urged against one's position. After all, we cannot "have our cake and eat it too."

The Problems with Modern Astrology

1. *Confusion*

Modern astrology is in a state of confusion and self-contradiction. Astrologers are literally tearing each other's horoscopes to pieces because they are drawing up conflicting horoscopes for the same person.

They argue over such questions as, Should we use the tropical or sidereal zodiac? When did the age of Aquarius begin, in 1904, 1936, 1962, 1999, etc.? Is Saturn an *evil* influence or an influence for *justice*? Is the influence of the stars of a *physical* or *astral* nature? Are there really *twelve* houses or only *eight*? Should the zodiac conform to the constellations?

The astrologers have yet to find a proper method for drawing the houses in a chart. Cavendish observes:

> Some use the system invented by Camparius in the eleventh century, others the system invented by Rigiomontanus in the fifteenth century, and others have devised their own methods. Some begin the first house with the ascendant, others begin it near but not at the ascendant. Some space the houses evenly so that each house covers 30 degrees of the zodiac, but others space the houses unevenly. The inevitable result is that different astrologers give different interpretations of the same planetary position, because they place the planets in different houses.[11]

Some astrologers repudiate the astrological columns in the daily newspapers and call it "slop" astrology. They also reject *Linda Goodman's Sun Signs* and other "pop" astrological works which base their readings on the position of the sun at the time of birth.

> All serious astrologers agree that newspaper or so-called "Sun Sign" astrology is nonsense. (President of National Astrological Society)[12]
> The serious student of astrology does not condone the use of horoscope columns or magazines, since the basis of these prognostications are for sun signs only.[13]

Evidently, while "sun sign" astrology is popular with the masses, it is very unpopular with "serious" astrologers. Its claim to be a science must be rejected. No one actually knows which astrological system or method is the right one.

2. *Perpetuated Error*

The vast majority of astrologers have perpetuated the basic scientific and philosophic errors of Ptolemy. They are still using Ptolemy's geo-centered, seven-star zodiac of twelve houses according to the calculations in his *Tetrabiblos*. They are functioning as if no new planets were discovered and as if the precession of the equinox does not happen.

3. *An Expanding Universe*

The stars are not *fixed* but *moving* at tremendous speeds. The stars are speeding away from us and even "winking" out as they move. The astronomer Jastrow comments:

> We have been aware for fifty years that we live in an expanding universe, in which all the galaxies around us are moving apart from us and one another at enormous speeds. The universe is blowing up before our eyes.[14]

We are not aware of any astrologers who have grappled with the implications of the conflict between astrology's "fixed" universe and reality's expanding universe. Reason and scientific measurement tell us that the further away the stars and constellations move, the *less* influence they will have on us. Are we to believe that astrology's power over our lives is gradually weakening as the stars move away?

4. *Other Problems*

There are still other problems with modern astrology which should be identified:

A. Astrology is a mystical or magical explanation of a problem which has since been explained by the discovery of DNA and the development of the science of genetics. The ancient astrologers had no knowledge of genetics. They explained the physical and psychological characteristics of people as being determined solely *from above* by the stars. Modern science has discovered that such things are to a great degree the result of an interplay between genetic forces from *within*, environmental forces from *without*, and the free volitional decisions that the person makes in life.

B. Identical, fraternal and time twins should share the same kind of personality, career, experiences, and death. We saw in a previous chapter that twin studies militate against astrology.

C. Astrologers have never given any rational or scientific explanation why the time of birth is when a person's destiny is "fixed" by the stars. Why isn't *conception* the beginning of the star's influence? Why not *puberty*? Why is *birth* the crucial time?

No reason is given by astrologers for their choosing the *time* of birth as opposed to choosing the *place* of birth. After all, since the *locations* of the planets are the basis of the zodiac, should not the *location* of a person's birth be more important than the time of the birth? We can therefore conclude: modern astrologers *arbitrarily* use the time of birth instead of conception or its location because Ptolemy arbitrarily chose birth as the starting point. While the time of birth is convenient, this does not show that it is valid.

D. What about the problem of mass tragedies? Some astrologers have reluctantly admitted that mass tragedies pose a serious dilemma for their profession:

> Did all the Jews murdered by Hitler have death written into their horoscopes? . . . Astrologers contend that the individual's destiny is subsumed in the greater laws governing his city, state, nation or race. But astrologers are unable to distinguish satisfactorily the general from the particular, and perhaps were never able to.[15]

Natal astrology assumes that we can *know* a person's horoscope. Yet, mass tragedies render all natal horoscopes *invalid*. So, the astrologers point to mundane astrology which concerns the destiny of a nation as overruling natal horoscopes. If this is true, why are they in the business of only making up *natal* horoscopes? Why are there only a few mundane astrologers around today?

The few astrologers who do persist in casting horoscopes for the destiny of nations come up with results that "are unlikely to impress the scientist or statistician, nor will apparently arbitrary methods convince the skeptics."[16]

E. Belief in astrology has caused severe psychological harm to some people. For example, a woman went to an astrologer and obtained a horoscope for her son. After the astrologer revealed the supposed future of her son, she went home and killed him to save him from a worse fate.[17] One wonders, how many suicides and murders are the result of negative horoscopes?

How can the astrologers present their horoscopes as a *beneficial* science? It appeals only to those who want quick and easy answers, but who cannot psychologically handle what they get. If astrology were a science, it would be an evil one. As we have already seen, however, astrology is better classified as religion rather than science.

Chapter 4

A Philosophic Analysis

After the scientific revolution, astrology lost importance, because it was dismissed as mere superstition. People thought it would eventually die out as science progressed. However, astrology's basis and nature is really a religious philosophic world view. The present resurgent popularity of astrology warrants a preliminary philosophic analysis. This is not as easy as it might seem. One fails to find any extensive references to astrology in standard philosophic reference works. It has not been viewed as worthy of refutation or analysis by classic philosophers.[1]

Twelve Philosophic Questions

1. Therefore we must ask: *Does faith in astrology have any grounds in the world around us or in the nature of man himself? Is faith in astrology a totally subjective leap into the dark?*

In every philosophy there must be *faith* in the presuppositions upon which the philosophy rests. The faith which a person has in these philosophic first principles (which must be *assumed* to be true) may be:

  a. A complete leap into the dark without any reason.
  b. A choice of which presupposition he wishes to place his faith in on the basis of rational, empirical or other reasons.
  c. Ignorance of these assumptions and where they came

from. Too many people pick up their presuppositions like dogs pick up fleas.

On the basis of our research, the astrologer's faith is externally and internally groundless. Astrology is a leap into the dark.

2. *Are the presuppositions—the first principles—of astrology valid?*

Since the presuppositions of astrology are embedded in polytheistic planet worship and Ptolemy's geo-centered zodiac, they are not valid.

3. *Are there basic errors in the presuppositions of astrology that render the believer incapable of finding the truth?*

Astrology is built on the erroneous concept that appearance always corresponds to reality. The entire zodiac is built on this idea.

4. *Are the concepts of astrology consistent with, or contradictory to, its own presuppositions?*

Astrology presupposes that the zodiac is *real* and that it reflects the *actual* position of the stars. Modern astrologers contradict this view, saying that the zodiac should not be seen as a star map or a guide to the constellations. Yet, they still say that the zodiac is real, not just an optical illusion or myth, even though they admit that it does not correspond to reality.

5. *Do astrological concepts agree with or contradict each other?*

We have already pointed out that there are many conflicting and mutually contradicting concepts in astrology (e.g., tropical vs. sidereal zodiacs, 8 or 12 houses, etc.).

6. *Are the concepts of astrology coherent? Are they understandable as a whole and in their parts?*

The astrologers themselves admit that they do not understand astrology. They interpret the same planetary positions in different ways. Therefore, it is not a coherent philosophy.

7. *Are the concepts of astrology cohesive? Do they "hang" together or fit into one grand system?*

Astrology is an uncohesive "mixed bag" of conflicting presuppositions and concepts with no principle of unity.

8. *Are the concepts of astrology self-refuting? Do they carry within themselves the seeds of their own destruction?*

Astrology limits itself to *observable* stars and constellations as the basis for the zodiac and for drawing horoscopes on this zodiac. It was only a matter of time before other planets and stars would be discovered rendering all previous horoscopes invalid.

9. *Can the concepts of astrology stand up under rigorous exposure to the Law of Contradiction?*

The astrologers contradict themselves when it comes to the influences of Uranus, Neptune, and Pluto. Their disavowal of the precession of the equinox gives another example.

10. *Can the astrologers live what they believe and believe what they live?*

While speaking the majority of time in clearly *fatalistic* terminology and ascribing our personality, career, and even death to a destiny *determined* by the stars, they turn around at the last moment and claim that "the stars do not compel but impel."[3]

Evidently, they want to *talk* about their destiny being determined by the stars, but they are incapable of *living* in the light of such depressing fatalism.

11. *Are the concepts of astrology verifiable? Have they been verified? Do they correspond to reality?*

We have already reviewed numerous tests of astrology

which showed that it does not correspond to reality. The lack of the "Mars effect" in the horoscopes of criminals provides one example. That the zodiac is no longer based on the actual position of the stars gives another example.

12. *Where will this system ultimately take us if we allow it to be consistent, if we follow it to its logical conclusion?*

Astrology would ultimately make us the slaves of the astrologers. They would control our marriages, careers, even war. Modern medicine and psychology would be destroyed. Astrologers would tell us when and where to operate, and would blame all mental illness on the stars, particularly the moon. Business would collapse because workers would stay at home whenever the astrologers predicted a bad day. Astrologers would even tell us when to make love with our mate. Famine and starvation would spread as farmers waited for the astrologers to tell them if and when to plant.

Astrology is an all-consuming world view which can potentially dictate every aspect of our daily lives. Astrology would ultimately bring about the destruction of reason, hope, meaning, significance, and love.

Chapter Five

Is Astrology Christian?

The vast majority of astrologers claim to be "Christian" in some sense. Just as we have examined their claim to be "scientific," we must examine their claim to be "Christian."

"Christian" is a word which describes someone who believes in the teachings of Jesus Christ and the Apostles. These teachings are historical and biblical in nature. When someone departs from the doctrine or theology of historic and biblical Christianity, he should no longer use the word "Christian" to describe himself or his teaching. He should invent new terminology for his new religion.

Biblical Christianity cannot be limited to one particular church or denomination. It refers to all who embrace the theology of the historic creeds and confessions such as the Apostles' Creed, Nicene Creed, etc.

The theology of the historic creeds is carefully articulated and very clear as to what Christianity teaches. Essential Christian teaching refers to such doctrines as the Trinity, the deity of Christ, the virgin birth of Christ, Christ's death on the cross as a sacrifice for sin, His bodily resurrection and literal return to earth. Because of the clarity of the historic creeds, the Christian Church has been able to discern concepts which are radically anti-Christian. The Church has called anti-Christian teaching heresy and the group that follows the teaching a cult.

The touchstone of historic Christianity has always been the Gospel. What is this Gospel or good news?

> For what I received I passed on to you as of first impor-
> tance: that Christ died for our sins according to the Scrip-
> tures, that he was buried, that he was raised on the third day
> according to the Scriptures. (1 Cor. 15:3-4)
>
> For God so loved the world that he gave his one and only
> Son, that whoever believes in him shall not perish but have
> eternal life. (John 3:16)

The authors of the New Testament were deeply concerned
that the Gospel would not be corrupted or denied by anti-
Christian teaching. They commanded that false teaching be
condemned by the Church.

> But even if we or an angel from heaven should preach a
> gospel other than the one we preached to you, let him be eter-
> nally condemned! (Gal. 1:8)

It is from such a stance of historic and biblical Christianity
that we will examine the religious world view of astrology.

Astrology Is Hostile to Christianity

Even though the majority of astrologers claim to be Christian, they are generally hostile to the teachings of historic and
biblical Christianity. The teaching of several prominent astrologers will serve as examples.

The "Reluctant Prophet," D. Logan, states that Jesus is
not the Christ. He denies Noah's flood. He rejects the biblical
story of Adam and Eve. He speaks of a coming Antichrist with
approval. He says of one cult, "The teaching of Christian
Science is correct."[1]

Linda Goodman's books have been best-sellers. While she
herself may not claim to be Christian, she goes out of her way
to make statements which are hostile to Christianity. She denies that Jesus was the Christ, and states that He was only a
man. She suggests a return to male/female polytheism. She
even claims that the original sin of Adam and Eve was *good*
and not evil![2]

While Ms. Goodman is entitled to her beliefs, her beliefs

are not acceptable for anyone who claims to be a Christian. Her statements should be judged according to the standard the Apostle John sets forth:

> Who is the liar? It is the man who denies that Jesus is the Christ. Such a man is the antichrist—he denies the Father and the Son. (1 John 2:22)

Astrology and Reincarnation

Astrology's hostility to biblical Christianity reveals itself very clearly in its commitment to the theory of reincarnation.

The influence from the stars explains *how* each of us have our destinies fixed at birth. Most astrologers call upon the theory of reincarnation to explain *why* we all have different destinies.[3]

Astrological destinies are determined by one's karma.[4] One astrologer stated that through reincarnation, the soul picks the time of its rebirth to coincide with a particular arrangement of stars.[5]

According to the Scriptures, we have only this present life in which to prepare for eternity. Man's soul did not preexist his conception in the womb. He is not recycled in a numberless series of rebirths. Karma is a myth. The death of Christ on the cross paid the debt we owed to the law of God because of our sins. Christ's death in man's place renders karmic reincarnation as unnecessary as it is untrue.

Astrology Is Condemned by the Bible

We have already surveyed the numerous passages of Scripture in which astrology is condemned by God as an abomination. Since a Christian is one who believes in the Bible as God's Word, no Christian can believe in something God has condemned as error.

Some people argue that the Church has suppressed and excluded from the Canon certain "lost books." These supposedly indicate that Jesus believed in astrology and reincarnation. *The Unknown Life of Christ* and *The Aquarian Gospel* are the most well known of these books.

Dr. Edgar J. Goodspeed of the University of Chicago was one of the greatest New Testament scholars America ever produced. He examined in his book *Modern Apocrypha* (Beacon Press, Boston, 1956), *The Unknown Life of Christ* and *The Aquarian Gospel* and all the other so-called lost books of the Bible. He demonstrates that they are complete frauds. For example, some of the so-called lost books of the Bible written during the late Middle Ages describe Jesus and the Apostles as wearing items of clothing common only to the Middle Ages. They contain historically inaccurate information and fraudulent claims. Notovitch's claim that he received *The Unknown Life of Christ* from the chief Lama of the Monastery of Himis was investigated by a team who traveled to the monastery. The chief Lama swore by oath that Notovitch had never visited him. When Notovitch's book was read to the chief Lama he exclaimed, "Lies, lies, lies, nothing but lies."

Astrology Is Polytheistic

The original planetary worship of astrology still explains how the stars determine our destinies. The stars are viewed as deities who have the will and power to determine man's destiny.

By contrast, Christianity is wholly committed to monotheism. Therefore, Christians are not fooled by an ancient polytheistic religion just because it attempts to clothe itself in twentieth-century scientific terminology.

Astrology Is Occult

The word "occult" describes those tools, skills, and rites which the Bible forbids because they are satanic in origin and power.

When the Christian Church outlawed all occult practices because they were condemned by God in the Bible, all occult practices had to be done in secret to escape prosecution. Thus the Latin word *occultus*, which means "hidden" or "unseen," was used to describe them.

People become involved in occult practices such as astrology for one or all of the following reasons:

1. To gain supernatural knowledge of the future.
2. To gain supernatural power to affect the future and one's present condition.
3. To gain access to the spirit world to contact the dead for the living.
4. To contact Satan and the demonic host.

Astrology has always been, and still is, a branch of black witchcraft. Is it any wonder that the occult religions of our own day (e.g., the Church of Light, Rosicrucianism, Theosophy, etc.) are at the forefront of the astrological movement?

If astrology is not occultic, why do we find such astrologers as Daniel Logan involved with psychometry, séances, trances, mediums and spirits?[7] Why do West, Tooner and Russell connect the modern revival of astrology with the outbreak of spiritism in the late nineteenth century?[8] Why does Newall connect astrology with witchcraft, séances and spiritism?[9] Did not Dr. Dee practice crystal gazing?[10] If astrology is not occultic, why does it have talismans: zodiac jewelry such as rings, necklaces, medallions, pins, etc.?[11] Why do astrologers state that "psychic intuition" is necessary in drawing up accurate horoscopes?[12]

The only rational answer is that astrology is an occultic and magical art.

Astrology Is a Poor Substitute for Revelation

After all the years of scientific research and archaeological findings, the Bible has never once been shown by any empirical discoveries to be in error at any point. Whenever the Bible predicted an event, it came to pass.[13]

When you compare the failures and internal and external contradictions in astrology to the reliability of the Bible, astrology comes out the loser.

Moses laid down a rule concerning predictions which we should observe at this point:

> You may say to yourselves, "How can we know when a message has not been spoken by the Lord?" If what a prophet proclaims in the name of the Lord does not take place or come true, that is a message the Lord has not spoken. That prophet has spoken presumptuously. Do not be afraid of him. (Deut. 18:21, 22)

Moses points out that God's prophets *never* fail to predict the future accurately. Therefore, we can discover a false prophet quite easily. *One false prediction makes a false prophet.* The astrologers have failed repeatedly to predict the future. According to Moses, they are false prophets who will lead people into error.

Astrology Affords a Low View of Man

Astrology pictures man as the plaything of the stars which rule over every facet of his life.

How different is the biblical view of man. We are created in God's image. This image is not a *physical* correspondence, . . . for God is spirit, without flesh and bones (Num. 23:19; Luke 24:39; John 4:24). The image of God refers to certain capacities and capabilities man has which are reflective of God's nature and character.

When God created man, He placed him over the earth and gave him authority over the animals. Man has the responsibility of exercising dominion over the cosmos.

> So God created man in his own image, in the image of God he created him; male and female he created them. God blessed them and said to them, "Be fruitful and increase in number; fill the earth and subdue it. Rule over the fish of the

sea and the birds of the air and over every living creature that moves on the ground." (Gen. 1:27, 28)

Biblical Christians oppose all forms of determinism. Man is not a machine programmed by genetics or an animal conditioned by environment. Man is made in the image of God. While the world may influence him to some degree, it cannot completely control him or determine his destiny. Man is born free.

For the Christian, the stars' function is to "declare the glory of God" and "to show his handiwork" (Ps. 19:1); not to guide the destiny of man. It is *idolatry* to ascribe to the stars that which belongs *only* to the God who created them. It is sheer folly to look to the stars instead of to the Scriptures.

The words of Isaiah to the astrologers of his day are just as true today:

All the counsel you have received has only worn you out! Let your *astrologers* come forward, those stargazers who make predictions month by month, let them save you from what is coming upon you. Surely they are like stubble; the fire will burn them up. They cannot even save themselves from the power of the flame. Here are no coals to warm anyone; here is no fire to sit by. That is all they can do for you—these you have labored with and trafficked with since childhood. Each of them goes on in his error; there is not one that can save you. (Isa. 47:13-15)

Conclusion

The theory and practice of astrology has been examined in terms of its origin, history, popular arguments, scientific credibility, philosophic integrity, and its compatibility with historic and biblical Christianity. The theory of astrology fails to validate its claims to be scientific and philosophically credible. Its internal contradictions and the scientific evidence against it are conclusive to those who approach it with an open mind. Astrology is merely the modern form of ancient planetary worship. Its language and *raisoń d'etre* are clearly polytheistic and anthropomorphic. As a religious world view, it is incompatible with Christianity. It has been weighed in the scales of history, science, philosophy, and Christianity and has been found lacking of any validity. Its only appeal to modern man is by way of superstition and magic. There is no place for astrology in the life of a Christian believer.

Bibliography of Astrological Works Consulted

Astrology, ed. Lynch, Viking Press, N.Y., 1902.

Benjamine, E., *Beginners Horoscope*, The Church of Light, Ca., 1943.

Cavendish, R., *The Black Arts*, Capricorn Books, 1967.

Davison, R., *Astrology*, A.R.C. Books, N.Y., 1964.

Doane & Keyes, *Tarot-Card Spreader*, Parker Pub. Co., Inc., N.Y.

Gauquelin, M., *The Cosmic Clocks*, Henry Regency Co., N.Y., 1967.

———— *The Scientific Basis of Astrology*, Stein & Day, N.Y., 1969.

Glass, J., *They Forsaw the Future*, C. P. Putnam's Sons, N.Y., 1969.

Goodavage, J., Astrology—*The Space Age Science*, New American Library, N.Y., 1960.

Goodman, L., *Linda Goodman's Love Signs*, Harper & Row Pub., N.Y., 1978.

———— *Linda Goodman's Sun Signs*, Toplinger Pub. Co., N.Y., 1968.

Heindel M. & Heindel A., *The Message of the Stars*, The Rosicrucian Fellowship, 1963.

———— *Simplified Scientific Astrology*, The Rosicrucian Fellowship, 1928.

Howe, E., *Astrology*, Walker & Co., N.Y., 1968.

Leek, Sybil, *My Life in Astrology*, Prentice-Hall, Inc., N.J., 1972.

Logan, D., *The Anatomy of Prophecy*, Prentice-Hall, Inc., N.J.

———— *The Reluctant Prophet*, Doubleday & Co., N.Y., 1980.

———— *Your Eastern Star*, William Morrow & Co., N.Y., 1972.

Lyndoe, E., *Astrology for Everyone*, E. P. Dutton & Co., Inc., 1970.

Newall, V., *The Encyclopedia of Witchcraft & Magic*, Dial Press, N.Y., 1974.

Pagan, I., *From Pioneer to Poet*, Theosophical Pub. House, Ill., 1969.

Parker, D., *Astrology in the Modern World*, Toplinger Pub. Co., N.Y., 1976.

Rudhyar, D., *The Astrological Houses*, Doubleday & Co., N.Y., 1972.

Rudhyar, D., *The Astrology of America's Destiny*, Random House, N.Y., 1974.

Russell, E., 1974.

Russell, E., *Astrology and Prediction*, Drake Pub., N.Y., 1973.

Sakoian F. & Acker L., *The Astrologer's Handbook*, Harper & Row Pub., N.Y., 1973.

The Complete Prophecies of Nostradamus, tr. H.C. Roberts, Nostradamus, Inc. N.Y., 1978.

Van Deusen, E., *Astro-Genetics*, Doubleday & Co., Inc., N.Y., 1976.

West, J. & Tooner J., *The Case for Astrology*, Coward-McCann, Inc., N.Y., 1970.

Suggested Bibliography for Further Study

Chang, Lit Sen, *Zen-Existentialism*, Pres. & Ref. Pub. Co., N.J., 1961.

Goodspeed, E., *Modern Apocrypha*, Beacon Press, Boston, 1956.

Kurt, K., *Satan's Devices*, Kregel Pub., Mich., 1978.

Machen, G., *The Origin of Paul's Religion*, Wm. B. Eerdmans Pub. Co., Grand Rapids, 1965.

Mackay, C., *Extraordinary Popular Delusions*, L. C. Page & Co., Boston, 1932.

McDowell, J., *Evidence That Demands a Verdict*, Campus Crusade For Christ, Inc., 1979.

Montgomery, J., *Principalities and Powers*, Bethany House Pub., 1973.

Morey, R., *The Christian Handbook for Defending the Faith*, Pres. & Ref. Pub. Co., N.J., 1979.

———— *Reincarnation and Christianity*, Bethany House Pub., Minn., 1980.

———— *The Saving Work of Christ*, G.A.M., Sterling, Va., 1980.

Newport, J., *Demons, Demons, Demons*, Broadman Press, 1972.

Noorberger, R., *The Soul Hustlers*, Zondervan Pub. Co., Mich., 1976.

Petersen, W., *Those Curious New Cults*, Keats Pub., Inc., Conn., 1973.

Schaeffer, F., *He Is There and Is Not Silent*, Tyndale House Pub., Ill., 1972.

Unger, M., *Demons in the World Today*, Tyndale House Pub., Ill., 1971.

Wilburn, G., *The Fortune Sellers*, Regal, Ca., 1972.

Notes

NOTES TO CHAPTER ONE

1. Glass, J., *They Foresaw the Future*, C. P. Putnam's Sons, N.Y., 1969, p. 11.
2. Horoscope Guide, June 1980, A.J.B.H. Pub., p. 16. *International Standard Bible Encyclopedia*, ed. J. Orr, Wm. B. Eerdmans Pub. Co., Mich., 1934, Vol. I, pp. 298, 300.
3. Keil & Delitzsch, *Biblical Commentary on the Old Testament*, Wm. B. Eerdmans Pub., Co., Mich., n.d., Vol. II, p. 416.
4. See: *Englishman's Hebrew and Chaldee Concordance*, Appendix, p. 10, for all references to Baal in the Old Testament.
5. The worship of Astarte is referred to in the following passages: Ex. 34:13; Deut. 7:5; 12:3; 16:21-22; Judges 3:7; 6:25-32; 1 Kings 11:5; 14:15, 23; 15:13; 16:33; 18:19; 2 Kings 13:6; 17:10-16; 18:4; 21:3-7; 23:4-20; 2 Chron. 14:3; 15:16; 17:6; 19:3; 24:18; 31:1; 33:3, 19; 34:3-7; Isa. 17:8; 27:9; Jer. 17:2; Mic. 5:14.
Scholars are divided as to whether Astarte referred to the moon, the planet Venus, or both of them combined. For further research see:
Alexander, J., *Isaiah*, Zondervan Pub. Co., Mich., 1962, p. 336.
Laetsch, T., *The Minor Prophets*, Concordia Pub. House, Mo., 1956, p. 277.
Lange's Commentary, Zondervan Pub. Co., Mich., 1960: (Vol. 2 (Deut.), p. 99; Vol. 3 (2 Kings), pp. 169, 186; Vol. 6 (Isa.), p. 213).
Delitzsch, F., *Isaiah*, Wm. B. Eerdmans Pub. Co., Mich., 1967, p. 342.
6. Keil, C. F., *The Book of Kings*, Wm. B. Eerdmans Pub. Co., Mich., 1950, pp. 469-470.
7. Lange, ibid., Vol. 3 (2 Kings), p. 261.
8. Keil, C. F., *Biblical Commentary on the Prophecies of Ezekiel*, pp. 122-124.
9. I.S.B.E., Vol. I., p. 300.
10. Abell, G., Humanist, Jan./Feb. 1976, p. 34.

11. This is universally accepted.
    Davison, R., *Astrology*, A.R.C. Books Inc., N.Y., 1963, p. 15.
    Gauquelin, M., *The Scientific Basis of Astrology*, Stein & Day, N.Y., 1969, p. 96.
    Rudhyar, D., *The Astrology of America's Future*, Random House, N.Y., 1974, p. 8.
    Jerome, L., Humanist, Sept./Oct. 1975, p. 13.
12. *The Apostolic Fathers*, tr. J. B. Lightfoot, Baker Book House, Grand Rapids, Mich., 1956.
13. *The Confessions of Saint Augustine*, Collier Books, N.Y., 1966 pp. 50-51.
14. Astrology was penalized in England in the Witchcraft Act of 1735 and the Vagrancy Act of 1829.
15. Russell, E., *Astrology and Prediction*, Drake Pub., Inc., N.Y., 1973, pp. 80-81.
16. Newall, V., *The Encyclopedia of Witchcraft & Magic*, Dial Press, N.Y., 1974, p. 25.
17. Ibid., p. 24.
18. Russell, ibid., p. 98.
    Morey, R., *Reincarnation and Christianity*, Bethany House Pub., Minn., 1980, pp. 12-13.
19. Russell, ibid., p. 113.

NOTES TO CHAPTER TWO

1. Gauquelin, M., *The Scientific Basis of Astrology*, Stein & Day, N.Y., 1969, p. 132.
2. Van Deusen, *Astro-Genetics*, Doubleday & Company, Inc., N.Y., 1976, pp. 81, 124 ff.
3. Human Behavior, April 1975, p. 31.
4. Russell, ibid., pp. 115-117.
5. Gauquelin, M., ibid., p. 119.
6. Russell, ibid., pp. 152, 80, 88.
   Also see: Glass, J., *They Foresaw the Future*, C. P. Putnam's Sons, N.Y., 1969.
7. Cavendish, ibid., p. 206.
8. Unger, M., *Demons in the World Today*, Tyndale House Pub., Ill., 1971, p. 61.
9. Ibid., p. 9.
10. Russell, ibid., p. 60.
11. Ibid., p. 77.
12. Ibid., p. 91.
13. Ibid., p. 13.
    Noorberger, ibid., p. 175.
14. Russell, ibid., p. 114.

15. Ibid., pp. 115-117.
16. Goodavage, J., *Astrology: The Space Age Science*, Parker Pub. Co., N.Y., 1966, p. 211.
17. Gauquelin, M., ibid., p. 133.
18. Russell, ibid., p. 119.
19. Logan, D., *The Reluctant Prophet*, Doubleday & Company, N.Y., 1968, p. 207.
20. Noorberger, ibid., p. 18.
21. See: West, J. & Tooner, J., *The Case For Astrology*, Coward-McCann, Inc., N.Y., 1970, p. 190. MacRay, C., *Extraordinary Popular Delusions*, L. C. Page & Co., Boston 1932, pp. 265-267
22. *The Complete Prophecies of Nostradamus*, tr. by H. C. Roberts, Nostradamus, Inc., N.Y., 1978.
23. Mackay, ibid., p. 280.
24. *The Complete Prophecies of Nostradamus*, ibid., pp. 11,236.
25. Ibid., p. 342 (#91).
26. Ibid., p. 236.
27. Ibid., p. 265 (#7).
28. Ibid., p. 24 (#49).
29. Roberts' attempt to date from the council of Nicea when he wants to explain 1607, 1700, etc., is clearly "prejudiced" when he lets stand the date 1792 (p. 236) because he thinks it was fulfilled.
30. Russell, ibid., p. 73.
31. Ibid.
32. Russell, ibid., p. 28 ff.
    Goodavage, ibid., pp. x1, 43.
    Tyler, C., Horoscope Guide, June 1980, p. 8.
33. Russell, ibid., p. 28 ff.
34. Ibid., p. 55.
35. Ibid., p. 52. That Christianity did not develop out of this Greek mystery cult, see: Machen, G., *The Origin of Paul's Religion*, Wm. B. Eerdmans Pub. Co., Mich., 1965. The Apostle Paul wrote the New Testament book of Colossians to refute Gnosticism.
36. Goodavage, ibid., p. 43.
37. Ibid., p. xl.
38. Ibid.
39. Gauquelin, M., ibid., p. 124.
    Van Tine, E., Horoscope Guide, June 1980, p. 82.
    Pagan, I., *From Pioneer to Past*, Theosophical Press, Ill., 1969, p. IX.
40. Bouw, G., "On the Star of Bethlehem," Creation Research Soci-

ety Quarterly, Dec. 1980, Vol. 17, No. 3, p. 179.

41. Davison, ibid., p. 12.
    Goodavage, ibid., pp. 1-15.

42. Eriksen, W. Keith, "The Inaccuracy of Astrological Research," The Humanist, Nov./Dec. 1976, pp. 43-44.

43. Gauquelin, M., *The Cosmic Clocks*, Henry Regency Co., N.Y., 1967, p. 85.

44. *Strange Stories, Amazing Facts*, Reader's Digest Ass., Inc., 1976, p. 52.

45. Davison, ibid., p. 16. Gauquelin, M., Basis, p. 198. Goodavage, J., ibid., p. 40.

46. Davison, R., ibid., p. 11.
    Gauquelin, M., Clocks, p. 122 f.
    Gauquelin, M., Basis, p. 189 ff.
    Goodavage, J., ibid., p. 40.

47. Gauquelin, M., Cosmic Clocks, p. 122.
    Goodman, L., *Sun Signs*, Toplinger Pub. Co., N.Y., 1968, p. 541.
    Strange Stories, Amazing Facts, p. 52.

48. Ratzen, L., "The Astrology of the Delivery Room," The Humanist, Nov./Dec. 1975, p. 123.

49. Sagan, C., *Other Worlds*, Bantam Books, N.Y., 1975, p. 123.

50. *Los Angeles Times*, Sept. 14, 1975.

51. Benjamine, E., *Beginner's Horoscope*, The Church of Light, Ca., 1943.

52. Gauquelin, M., Clocks, p. 81.

53. Ibid., pp. 81-82.

54. Scientific Monthly, March 1941.

55. Gauquelin, M., ibid., p. 85.

56. J. I. R., June 20, 1973.

57. Gauquelin, M., ibid., p. 85.

58. Ibid., p. 82.

59. Montgomery, J., *Principalities and Powers*, Pyramid Pub., 1975, pp. 105-106.

60. Gauquelin, M., "The Influence of Planets on Human Beings," The Humanist, Jan./Feb. 1976, p. 29.

61. For further research, the debates between Gauquelin and the scientists connected with The Humanist and The Skeptical Inquirer should be consulted. The fact that Gauquelin has been willing to set aside his own statistical method and adopt one set up by Marvin Zeller has placed the conclusion of his work up in the air. The results are not published yet.

62. Gauquelin, ibid., pp. 81-82.

NOTES TO CHAPTER THREE

1. Goodavage, J., ibid., pp. 172-173.
2. Cavendish, ibid., p. 208.
3. West & Tooner, ibid., p. 134.
4. Cavendish, ibid., p. 191.
5. Gauquelin, ibid., p. 78.
6. Goodman, L., *Linda Goodman's Love Signs*, Harper & Row. Pub., N.Y., 1978. p. 20 f.
7. Le Gross, G., "The Aquarian Age," *Horoscope Guide*, June 1980, pp. 35-37.
8. Gauquelin, Basis, p. 131.
9. Cavendish, ibid., p. 191.
10. Le Gross, ibid., pp. 35-36.
11. Cavendish, ibid., p. 201.
12. The Humanist, Nov./Dec. 1975, p. 24.
13. Russo & Bermingham, The Humanist, Nov./Dec. 1975, p. 24.
14. Jastrow. R., *God and the Astronomers*, Reader's Library, Inc., Canada, 1978, p. 13.
15. West & Tooner, ibid., p. 141.
16. West & Tooner, ibid., p. 141.
17. Newport, ibid., p. 104.

NOTES TO CHAPTER FOUR

1. *The Encyclopedia of Philosophy* does not deal with astrology as a separate subject of analysis but refers to it only a few times as a biographical note in someone's life.
Windelband, *A History of Philosophy*, vol. II, p. 373 f., states that "Astrology, with its influence of the stars upon human life, the interpretation of dreams and signs, necromancy, with its conjunctions of spirits, the predictions of persons in the ecstatic state—all these elements of the Stoic and Neo-Platonic divination were then in luxuriant bloom" (reference to the Dark Ages). Copleston, S. J., in his *A History of Philosophy*, vol. 2, Part II, p. 166, mentions astrology only as a biographical note on Roger Bacon. Astrology has not been the subject of much philosophic analysis.
2. Morey, R., *A Christian Handbook for Defending the Faith*, Pres. & Ref. Pub. Co., N.J., 1979. In this book, eighteen philosophic questions are developed which can be applied to any philosophic worldview. How biblical Christianity satisfies all the questions is also set forth in this book.
3. *Linda Goodman's Sun Signs*, p. 547.

NOTES TO CHAPTER FIVE

1. Logan, D., ibid., pp. 200, 202, 209.
2. Goodman, L., *Love Signs*, ibid., pp. 8, 20, 21.
3. According to one survey, over 75% of the astrologers in the U.S. believe in reincarnation. See: Davison, *Astrology*, p. 12.
   Logan, D., *Your Easter Star*, p. 38. Pagan, ibid., p. XIII. Astrology, ed. Lynch, p. 17.
   Parker, D., *Astrology in the Modern World*, pp. 54-57, 103, 130.
4. Goodman, L., *Love Signs*, p. 12.
5. Aher, D., *St. Paul Dispatch*, Sept. 18, 1975.
6. See: Cavendish, *The Black Arts*, p. 219 f.
   Leek, S., *My Life in Astrology*, Prentice-Hall, Inc., N.J., 1972.
7. Logan, *Relectant Prophet*, pp. 63, 64, 65, 169, 170.
8. West & Tooner, ibid., p. 101.
9. *Encyclopedia of Witchcraft and Magic*, p. 65.
10. Russell, ibid., p. 81.
11. Cavendish, ibid., p. 219.
12. Davison, ibid., p. 138.
13. The Bible does not contradict itself and has never been shown to contain any factual errors of history or science. For further research see: McDowell, J., *Evidence That Demands a Verdict*, Campus Crusade For Christ, Inc., 1979.
    Schaeffer, F., *He Is There and Is Not Silent*, Tyndale House Pub., Ill., 1972.
    Schaeffer, F., No Final Conflict, Inter-Varsity Press, Ill., 1975.
    Can I Trust My Bible?, Moody Press, Chicago, 1968.
    Morey, R., *A Christian Handbook for Defending the Faith*, Pres. & Ref. Pub., Co., N.J., 1979.